Published by Ice House Books

JOLLY AWESOME is the design studio of London-based illustrator Matt Nguyen.
His collections are inspired by his love of Americana, British pop-culture and stuff that makes him smile.

Illustrated by JOLLY AWESOME
Designed by Richard Peck

p8 Teri Virbickis / shutterstock.com
p12 Nataliya Arzamasova / shutterstock.com
p15 Anna Hoychuk / shutterstock.com
p17 Arina P Habich / shutterstock.com
p18 MShev / shutterstock.com
p20 Elena Shashkina / shutterstock.com
p23 Kiian Oksana / shutterstock.com
p25 Monarexx / shutterstock.com
p26 Baconstudiony / shutterstock.com
p.31 Elena Shashkina / shutterstock.com
p.33 boombox / shutterstock.com
p35 Ryzhkov Photography / shutterstock.com

p37 Irina Sokolovskaya / shutterstock.com
p39 Jenny Pierce Photos / shutterstock.com
p41 Anna_Pustynnikova / shutterstock.com
p42 Julie Marshall / shutterstock.com
p45 theerakit / shutterstock.com
p46 Savinova Iuliia
p51 Brent Hofacker / shutterstock.com
p53 Rak kaa / shutterstock.com
p55 beebatch_photgraphy / shutterstock.com
p57 Signe Leth / shutterstock.com
p58 KITTY650 / shutterstock.com
p60 j_fisher / shutterstock.com

Ice House Books is an imprint of Half Moon Bay Limited
The Ice House, 124 Walcot Street, Bath, BA1 5BG
www.halfmoonbay.co.uk

ISBN 978-1-912867-02-8

Printed in China

JOLLY AWESOME
TASTES LIKE MAGIC

ICE HOUSE BOOKS

CONTENTS

WHAT AN ICE RAINBOW!

Ingredients

200 g (7 oz) caster sugar
225 ml (7.9 fl oz) water
2 tbsp light golden syrup
Food colouring of your choice
500 ml (17.6 fl oz) cranberry juice
500 ml (17.6 fl oz) lemonade
250 ml (8.8 fl oz) orange juice
Ice-lolly mould
Wooden ice-lolly sticks

Makes: approx. 12 x 100 ml lollies
Prep time: 10 minutes
Freeze time: 8 hours

Method

1. To make the sugar-syrup base, heat the sugar and water in a medium-sized saucepan at a medium heat. Once boiling, stir to dissolve the sugar. Take off the heat and add golden syrup whilst stirring. Leave to cool.

Continued on the next page.

2. Making the coloured layers:

Red: Add two tablespoons of sugar syrup and two drops of red food colouring to 250 ml (8.4 fl oz) of cranberry juice.

Orange: Add two tablespoons of sugar syrup, one drop of red food colouring and one drop of yellow food colouring to 250 ml (8.4 fl oz) of orange juice.

Yellow: Add two tablespoons of sugar syrup and two drops of yellow food colouring to 250 ml (8.4 fl oz) of lemonade.

Green: Add two tablespoons of sugar syrup and two drops of green food colouring to 250 ml (8.4 fl oz) of lemonade.

Purple: Add two tablespoons of sugar syrup, two drops of blue and one drop of red food colouring to 250 ml (8.4 fl oz) of cranberry juice.

3. Add 1 cm (⅓ inch) of red syrup mixture to each ice-lolly mould. Freeze for 30 minutes. Next add 1 cm (⅓ inch) of orange syrup mixture and freeze for another 30 minutes.

4. Now place a wooden lolly stick in the centre of each mould and add 1 cm (⅓ inch) of yellow syrup mixture. Freeze for 30 minutes.

5. Repeat the steps with the green and purple mixtures until the moulds are full. Then put the lollies into the freezer for a minimum of 3 hours.

6. When they are ready, remove the lollies from their moulds – pouring hot water around the outside will help to release them. Now enjoy the rainbows!

ALL THE VEG

Ingredients

1 large naan flatbread
1 tbsp tomato purée
1 tbsp red pesto
75 g (2.6 oz) grated mozzarella
½ large red pepper
1 medium carrot
½ tin of sweet corn
¼ small broccoli
¼ small red cabbage

Makes: 1 pizza
Prep time: 5 minutes
Cook time: 15 minutes

Method

1. Preheat the oven to 180°C/350°F. Chop all your vegetables into uniformly small pieces so they'll all have a similar cooking time.

2. Place the naan flatbread on a baking tray. Mix together the tomato purée and red pesto then spread on the flatbread. Sprinkle the grated mozzarella over the base sauce, then add the uncooked vegetables in a rainbow pattern on top.

3. Place in the oven and cook until the edges of the flatbread are golden brown, or until the vegetables are cooked just how you like them. Tuck in straight away.

SKEW
COMPLETE ME

Ingredients

1 orange pepper
1 yellow pepper
1 red onion
10 small mushrooms
2 small courgettes
4 green chillies
10 small orange tomatoes
10 cherry tomatoes
2 tbsp olive oil
8 skewers

Makes: 8 skewers
Prep time: 10 minutes
Cook time: 6–8 minutes

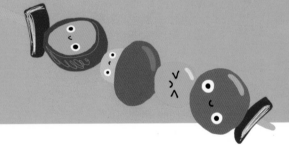

Method

1. Preheat the grill to a high temperature. Dice the peppers, chillies, red onion
    and courgettes into medium-sized pieces (make them around the same size
    as the cherry tomatoes and mushrooms).

2. Place the vegetables on the skewers in a pretty colour order and brush with olive oil.

3. Grill the skewers for 6–8 minutes, turning them to ensure even cooking. Enjoy immediately.

FRUITY TART

Ingredients

18-inch pastry case
250 ml (8.8 fl oz) whole milk
75 g (2.6 oz) caster sugar
2 tbsp plain flour
3 medium free-range egg yolks, beaten
1 tsp vanilla extract
1 punnet of blackberries
½ punnet of strawberries, cut into halves
1 kiwi, cut into slices
½ punnet of blueberries
80 g (2.8 oz) apricot jam
2 tbsp water

Makes: 1 tart
Prep time: 15 minutes

Method

1. To make the crème pâtissière filling, warm the milk and vanilla extract on a low-medium heat in a large saucepan.

2. In a large bowl, whisk the egg yolks, sugar and flour until the mixture becomes pale.

3. Slowly add the warm milk and vanilla to the egg mixture, whisking constantly.

4. Once blended, pour the mixture back into the saucepan and warm over a low heat until it thickens. Then pour into a large, clean bowl and place greaseproof paper on the top to prevent a skin forming.

5. Once the crème pâtissière has cooled, pour it into the pastry case and smooth out to fill the base. Decorate the top with the fruit.

6. Warm the apricot jam in a small saucepan with two tablespoons of water, then brush over the fruit to glaze.

7. Place your tart in the fridge until nice and cool, then serve.

RAINBOW PANCAKE STACK

Ingredients

135 g (5 oz) plain flour
½ tsp salt
1 tsp baking powder
2 tbsp caster sugar
130 ml (4.5 fl oz) semi-skimmed milk
1 large free-range egg, lightly beaten
2 tbsp butter, melted and allowed to cool slightly
Extra butter for greasing the pan
Food colouring of your choice
Vanilla ice cream and rainbow sprinkles, to serve

Makes: approx. 12 pancakes
Prep time: 10 minutes
Cook time: 10 minutes

Method

1. In a large bowl, sift together the flour, salt, baking powder and sugar. In a separate bowl, lightly whisk together the milk and egg, then whisk in the butter.

2. Add the milk mixture to the flour mixture and beat together until you have a smooth batter.

3. Divide the batter into six small bowls and add different food colouring to each bowl. Make sure you add a generous amount to achieve intense colours.

4. Heat a frying pan over a medium heat and melt a little butter into it. Then spoon a large dollop of batter into the centre of the pan. Leave for 1–2 minutes, until bubbles appear and the edges go slightly dry, then flip it over. Cook for another 1–2 minutes on the other side.

5. Keep your cooked pancakes in a slightly warm oven until you've made them all. Then pile them up to create your rainbow stacks. Top with a spoonful of ice cream and some rainbow sprinkles!

SUPER SANGRIA

Ingredients

1 punnet of blueberries
½ punnet of strawberries
½ punnet of grapes
3 kiwis
½ cantaloupe melon
½ pack of frozen mango
1½ bottles of white wine
125 ml (4.4 fl oz) triple sec
Juice of 3 limes
65 g (2.3 oz) sugar

Makes: 6 large glasses
Prep time: 15 minutes

Method

1. Dice the kiwi, melon and strawberries into small pieces.

2. In six large glasses, layer the grapes, blueberries, kiwi, mango, melon and strawberries to create a rainbow pattern.

3. In a large bowl, stir together the white wine, triple sec, lime juice and sugar.

4. Pour the cocktail over the layered fruit and serve.

SLAY THE SLAW

Ingredients

60 ml (2.1 fl oz) honey
60 ml (2.1 fl oz) lime juice
2 tbsp vinegar
1 tbsp ground cumin
½ tsp salt
¼ tsp ground pepper
70 ml (2.5 fl oz) olive oil
600 g (21.2 oz) red cabbage, shredded
2 courgettes, thinly sliced
2 red peppers, thinly sliced
2 carrots, grated
1 large handful of cress
2 tbsp sesame seeds

Makes: Serves 8
Prep time: 20 minutes

Method

1. Whisk the honey, lime juice, cumin, vinegar, and salt and pepper in a small bowl whilst slowly adding the olive oil.

2. In a separate bowl, combine the red cabbage, courgettes, red pepper, carrots and cress.

3. Pour the dressing over the vegetables and mix until everything is coated. Sprinkle with sesame seeds and serve.

UNICORN CHEESECAKE

Ingredients for base
125 g (4.4 oz) biscuits
¼ tsp salt
2 tsp brown sugar
60 g (2.1 oz) butter, melted

Makes: 1 cheesecake
Prep time: 20 minutes
Chilling time: 6 hours minimum

Ingredients for topping
800 g (28 oz) cream cheese
130 g (4.5 oz) icing sugar
1 tbsp vanilla extract
380 ml (12.8 fl oz) double cream
Food colouring in 3 colours of your choice
Edible pearls and rainbow sprinkles, to serve

Method for the base

1. In a food processor, blend the biscuits, salt and brown sugar until you have a fine consistency. Gradually add the melted butter, blending as you go.

2. Line a medium cake tin with greaseproof paper, then use a spoon to press your base mixture into the bottom of the tin. Place in the fridge to cool.

24

Method for the topping

1. Put the cream cheese, icing sugar and vanilla extract in a bowl and beat with an electric mixer until smooth. Add the double cream and continue mixing until completely combined.

2. Divide the topping into three bowls and add a few drops of different food colouring to each.

3. Pour the first colour layer onto the biscuit base and freeze for 30 minutes. Repeat for the second layer.

4. After your third layer is added, put the cheesecake in the fridge to chill for at least five hours (or overnight).

5. Once set, decorate with edible pearls and rainbow sprinkles to serve.

SOMEWHERE OVER THE BAGEL

Ingredients

220 ml (7.7 fl oz) warm water
½ tbsp sugar
1 tsp active dry yeast
660 g (23.3 oz) plain flour
½ tbsp oil
1 tsp salt
Food colouring of your choice

Makes: 4 bagels
Prep time: 1 hour 50 minutes
Cook time: 15 minutes

Method

1. In a large bowl (or food mixer) mix the warm water and sugar. Add the yeast and let the mixture stand until it starts to bubble (approx. 10 minutes).

2. Add the flour, oil and salt. Mix with a wooden spoon until thick. Move the dough to a flat, floured surface and knead by hand for five minutes until smooth. Sprinkle the dough with flour if it is too sticky.

3. Grease a large bowl with oil and put the dough in. Cover with cling film and set aside until the dough has doubled in size (this should take around one hour).

4. Once risen, divide the dough into at least three portions ready to be coloured. Dye each portion with food colouring to create your rainbow.

Continued on the next page.

5. Knead each portion for 10 minutes more, to ensure the colour will be even. Roll out each coloured dough ball into a rectangle and stack them in your chosen colour order. Twist the stack together to make a swirled log, then divide it into four balls.

6. To make a bagel shape, put a hole in the centre of each dough ball and stretch the mixture out slightly. Cover the bagels and set aside for 10 minutes to rise.

7. Preheat the oven to 230°C/450°F. Bring a large saucepan of water to the boil and drop in the bagels in batches for 1 minute, turning half way through.

8. Allow the bagels to dry and then bake for 15 minutes on a baking tray lined with greaseproof paper.

9. Allow to cool, then serve!

RAINBOW ROLLS

Ingredients for the ginger peanut sauce
600 ml (20 fl oz) of water
100 g (3.5 oz) peanut butter
1½ tbsp soy sauce
2 tbsp brown sugar
Juice of ½ a lime
½ tsp chilli garlic sauce
½ tsp grated ginger

Ingredients for the spring rolls
8 rice papers
½ red pepper, thinly sliced
½ yellow pepper, thinly sliced
2 large carrots, thinly sliced
1 large bunch of mint leaves
½ cucumber, thinly sliced
¼ red cabbage, shredded

Makes: 8 rolls
Prep time: 30 minutes

Method

1. To make the sauce, first boil the water then set aside to cool slightly.

2. In a small bowl, whisk together the peanut butter, soy sauce, brown sugar, lime juice, chilli garlic sauce and grated ginger. Add hot water, one tablespoon at a time, until the mixture has thinned to a dipping-sauce consistency.

3. To make the spring rolls, warm your rice papers by placing them in a shallow dish of hot water for 10–20 seconds each.

4. Transfer your warm rice papers onto a clean surface and smooth out into a circle. Add a mixed handful of the chopped vegetables in the centre and roll the rice paper around them. Press the paper together to seal.

5. Place your ginger peanut sauce into a small dipping bowl, and serve.

MAGICARONS

Ingredients

3 large free-range egg whites
50 g (1.8 oz) caster sugar
200 g (7 oz) icing sugar
110 g (3.9 oz) ground almonds
Food colouring of your choice
110 g (3.9 oz) white chocolate
30 g (1.1 oz) double cream

Makes: 50 macarons
Prep time: 35 minutes
Cook time: 13 minutes

Method

1. Preheat the oven to 140°C/285°F. Beat the egg whites with an electric whisk until they are foamy. Then beat in the caster sugar until the mixture becomes glossy and forms soft peaks.

2. Sift the icing sugar and ground almonds into a separate bowl, then quickly fold into the egg mixture.

3. Create a piping bag by cutting the corner off a clean plastic bag. Test your mixture by adding a small amount to the bag and piping a 4 cm (1½ inch) circle onto a lined baking tray. The circle should flatten immediately. If it stays in a peak, return to the mixture and gently fold a few more times.

4. When your mixture is ready, separate it into several bowls and add different food colourings. Then put the mixtures into different piping bags.

5. Pipe 4 cm (1½ inch) circles onto your baking tray and bake for 13 minutes, turning halfway through. Once ready, leave to cool.

6. Place the white chocolate and double cream in a small bowl and microwave for 30 seconds to melt. Mix fully, then divide into portions and add different food colourings. Place in the fridge until completely cooled down.

7. Once your macarons are also completely cool, add your fillings – and enjoy.

SUNSHINE & SUSHI

Ingredients

250 g (8.8 oz) sushi rice
3 tbsp sushi vinegar
3 sheets of nori (dried seedweed)
Small fillet of salmon
Small fillet of tuna
Small fillet of sea bass

1 avocado
1 cucumber
1 carrot
1 yellow pepper
1 raw beetroot
Soy sauce, to serve

Makes: 20 portions
Prep time: 15 minutes

Rolling mat and cling
film also required

Method

1. Cook the sushi rice as instructed on the packet, then add the sushi vinegar to it and leave to cool.

2. Thinly cut the fillets of fish into slices, 2.5 cm (1 inch) wide and long enough to sit over the top of each roll. Slice open and peel the avocado, then use a peeler to cut thin slices. Set aside.

3. Prepare your fillings – cut your remaining avocodo plus the cucumber, carrot, pepper and beetroot into very thin, long strips.

4. Lay one sheet of nori on a flat surface. Cover with a thin layer of sushi rice, pressing down so it sticks.

5. Now flip the nori over, onto your rolling mat, so the rice side is facing down. Pile your filling strips in a horizontal line across the nori sheet, about a third of the way up from the bottom.

6. Now roll the mat away from you to make one tight, long sushi roll.

7. Place your slices of fish and avocado over the roll, then cover with cling film and squeeze the roll together.

8. Remove the cling film and slice your roll into colourful portions.

MAKE ME POP

DUDE, SWEET!

Ingredients

180 g (6.3 oz) popcorn kernels/maize
2–3 tbsp vegetable oil
180 g (6.3 oz) fine sugar
2 tbsp water
Food colouring of your choice

Makes: approx. 5 servings
Prep time: 15 minutes

Method

1. Place the kernels and oil in a large saucepan. Cover and turn the heat up high.

2. Shake the pan as the kernels begin to pop. When the popping has stopped, remove the pan from the heat.

3. In a small saucepan, add the sugar and water and bring to the boil, stirring frequently until all the sugar has dissolved. Divide the sugar syrup into several bowls (one for each colour) and add a teaspoon of food colouring to each bowl.

4. Add a handful of popcorn to each bowl and use a spoon to fully coat the pieces in the coloured sugar syrups.

5. Allow the popcorn to dry, then mix together in a large bowl of rainbow joy!

RAINBOW
PRETZEL STICKS

Ingredients

1 pack of pretzel sticks
150 g (5.2 oz) white chocolate
30 g (1.1 oz) each of various coloured
decorating sugar or sprinkles

Makes: Lot of sticks!
Prep time: 10 minutes

Method

1. Cover a baking sheet with greaseproof paper. Carefully pour the sugar in rows across the paper, creating rainbow stripes.

2. Chop up the white chocolate and melt it in a bowl in the microwave, stirring at 10-second intervals until fully melted.

3. Dip the pretzel sticks into the white chocolate so two thirds of them are covered. Then immediately roll across the coloured sugar, creating stripes around your pretzel sticks.

4. Leave the coated pretzels on a clean piece of baking paper to dry before serving.

SMOOTHIE OPERATOR

Ingredients

Water for blending all smoothies

Red smoothie:
1 frozen banana
170 g (5.9 oz) Greek yoghurt
170 g (5.9 oz) frozen raspberries
170 g (5.9 oz) frozen strawberries

Orange smoothie:
1 frozen banana
170 g (5.9 oz) Greek yoghurt
170 g (5.9 oz) frozen peaches
1 small orange
85 g (2.9 oz) frozen mango

Yellow smoothie:
2 frozen bananas
170 g (5.9 oz) Greek yoghurt
240 g (8.5 oz) frozen pineapple

Green smoothie:
2 frozen bananas
170 g (5.9 oz) Greek yoghurt
1 handful spinach
170 g (5.9 oz) frozen pineapple

Purple smoothie:
1 frozen banana
170 g (5.9 oz) Greek yoghurt
170 g (5.9 oz) mixed frozen berries

Makes: 3-4 cups of each colour smoothie
Prep time: up to 10 minutes per juice

Method

1. It's easy to bring smooth colour joy to your life! For each smoothie, put all the ingredients in a blender and mix until smooth, rinsing the blender between colours.

2. Pour the different coloured smoothies into separate glasses, or you can layer them in the same glass.

   Tip: use a cocktail stick and swirl the layers together for a cool tie-dye effect!

FUN JUICE.

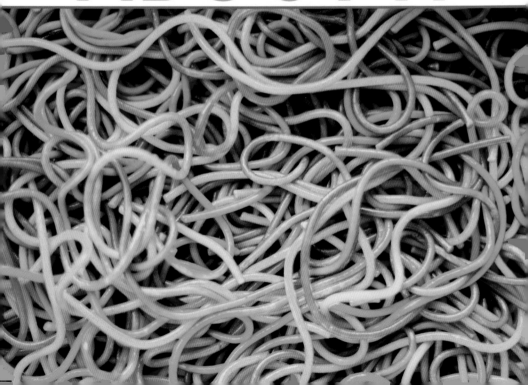

Ingredients

1 pack of dried spaghetti
Food colouring of your choice
Freezer bags (one for each colour)

Makes: 4 servings
Prep time: 20 minutes
Cook time: approx. 8–12 minutes

Method

1. In a large pan of boiling water, cook the spaghetti al dente, following the instructions on the packaging.

2. While the spaghetti is cooking, take as many freezer bags as you have colours, and add two tablespoons of water and around 20 drops of food colouring to each one.

3. Once the spaghetti is cooked, drain it in a colander and rinse with cold water.

4. Divide the cooked spaghetti into the freezer bags and seal them. Move the spaghetti around in the bag to ensure the colouring is evenly distributed.

5. Once all the spaghetti is coloured, rinse again in cold water, still keeping the colours separate.

6. Now you can mix all the spaghetti together to create a beautifully snazzy bowl.

OH CREPE!

Ingredients for crepes

140 g (4.9 oz) flour
3½ tbsp sugar
3 large free-range eggs
3 tbsp butter, melted
350 ml (12.3 fl oz) milk
Food colouring of your choice

Ingredients for filling

165 ml (5.5 oz) double cream
25g (1 oz) icing sugar
2 drops vanilla extract

Makes: 1 pancake stack
Prep time: 10 minutes
Cook time: 15 minutes

Method

1. Whisk the flour and sugar together in a large bowl. Add the eggs and slowly pour in the butter and milk while mixing, until you have a smooth batter.

2. Divide the batter into a bowl for each colour and add food colouring – mixing thoroughly.

3. Heat a frying pan over a medium heat and melt a little butter into it. Pour in enough batter to cover the bottom of the pan. Allow to cook for two minutes on each side. Repeat to make all your crepes.

4. For the whipped cream filling, put the cream, icing sugar and vanilla in a large bowl and whip until medium-stiff peaks form.

5. Once all the crepes are cooled, stack them on a serving plate with layers of whipped cream icing in between. Cover the top and sides with the icing, too, then cut into colourful pieces to serve.

SUCK IT & SEE

Ingredients for cake base

100 g (3.5 oz) butter
100 g (3.5 oz) caster sugar
½ tsp vanilla extract
2 large free-range eggs
100 g (3.5 oz) self-raising flour

Makes: approx. 12
Prep time: 45 minutes
Cook time: 20 minutes

Ingredients for icing and decoration

75 g (2.6 oz) butter
150 g (5.3 oz) icing sugar
½ tsp vanilla extract
1 tbsp milk
200 g (7.1 oz) milk chocolate
Rainbow sprinkles

Method

1. Preheat the oven to 190°C/375°F and grease and line two shallow sandwich cake tins.

2. To make the cake base, first beat together the butter, sugar and vanilla extract until creamy. Then beat in the eggs and fold in the flour until evenly mixed. Divide the mixture into the two cake tins and bake for 20 minutes until golden brown. Leave to cool on a wire rack.

3. To make the icing, beat the butter and icing sugar together in a large bowl. Add the vanilla extract and milk and continue to beat until smooth.

4. When the cake has completely cooled, crumble it up and mix thoroughly into the butter cream. Then take chunks out of the mixture and roll into small balls.

Continued on the next page.

5. Stick a lollypop stick halfway through each ball and place them on a tray in the fridge, with the sticks pointing upwards, for an hour.

6. Chop up the milk chocolate and melt gradually in the microwave in 10-second bursts, stirring regularly.

7. Dip your cake balls into the melted chocolate so they are completely covered. Then dip them into a bowl of rainbow sprinkles to decorate.

8. Return your pops to the fridge until they are completely cooled and the chocolate is hardened. Then enjoy!

YOU'RE SO SLUSH

Ingredients

Lots of ice pops in different colours

Makes: 1 big slush bowl (or several glasses)
Prep time: 5 minutes

Method

1. This is a very simple treat for a unicorn party. Simply take your frozen ice pops in various flavours, bash them until they turn to slush, and layer in a bowl to create a rainbow delight!

2. You could also layer the colours into separate glasses for your guests, and add paper straws.

RAINBOASTIE

Ingredients

2 slices of bread
110 g (3.9 oz) cheddar cheese, grated
Food colouring of your choice
1 tbsp butter

Makes: 1 toastie
Prep time: 15 minutes
Cook time: 12 minutes

Method

1. Divide the grated cheese into six small bowls and add different coloured food colouring to each bowl. Mix until the cheese is fully coated.

2. Place the coloured cheese in vertical lines on one of the pieces of bread, being careful not to mix the colours.

3. Place the other piece of bread on top and butter the outside of the sandwich.

4. Put the sandwich in a pan over a medium heat for two minutes, then flip and cook the other side. Remove from the heat, cut in half and serve. (Tip: a sandwich toaster works too!)

BABYCAKES

Ingredients for the cake

130 g (4.6 oz) softened butter
300 g (10.6 oz) caster sugar
5 large free-range egg whites
1 tbsp vanilla extract
390 g (13.8 oz) flour
4 tsp baking powder
½ tsp salt
145 ml (5.1 fl oz) milk
Food colouring of your choice

Makes: 24 cupcakes
Prep time: 30 minutes
Cook time: 20 minutes

Ingredients for the buttercream

130 g (4.6 oz) butter
1 tbsp vanilla extract
3 tbsp milk
520 g (18.3 oz) icing sugar

Method

1. Preheat the oven to 180°C/360°F. In a large bowl, beat together the butter and sugar, and then add the egg whites and vanilla extract until fully combined.

2. Sift in the flour, baking powder and salt then gradually mix in the milk.

3. Divide the mixture into several different bowls and add a few drops of food colouring to each bowl.

4. Prepare a cupcake tray with individual cases, then add a layer of each colour to each case until half full (they will rise).

5. Bake for 18–20 minutes until the tops are springy. Leave to cool completely.

6. To make the buttercream, whip the butter until it turns pale. Add the vanilla and milk. Gradually sift and whisk in the icing sugar until light and fluffy.

7. Once the cupcakes are cool, decorate with the buttercream and serve.

BECAUSE CAKE.

FRUITY RAINBOWL

Ingredients

1 frozen banana
510 g (17.9 oz) frozen strawberries
170 ml (5.9 fl oz) coconut milk
Different coloured fruits –
blueberries, blackberries, kiwi, mango,
strawberries, passionfruit

Makes: 1 bowl
Prep time: 5 minutes

Method

1. Place the banana, strawberries and coconut milk in a blender and mix until smooth and thick.

2. Pour the smoothie mixture into a large bowl and add your colourful fruity topping. Allow to chill in the fridge before serving.

MAGIC PEAK
MERINGUES

Ingredients

3 large free-range egg whites
175 g (6.2 oz) caster sugar
½ tbsp vanilla extract
Food colouring of your choice

Makes: 12 meringue swirls
Prep time: 30 minutes
Cook time: 1 hour 15 minutes

Method

1. Preheat the oven to 140°C/280°F. In a large bowl, whisk the egg whites until soft peaks form. While continuing to whisk, slowly add the caster sugar (1 tablespoon at a time) until the mixture is stiff and glossy. Whisk in the vanilla extract.

2. Divide the mixture into separate bowls and add different food colourings. Lightly mix to ensure even colouring.

3. Pour the coloured meringue mixtures into piping bags and create circular spirals on a lined baking tray, with little peaks for a pretty effect.

4. Bake for 1 hour 15 minutes then transfer to a wire rack to cool. Then tuck in!

HARD ROCK
COLOUR POPS

Ingredients

470 ml (16.5 fl oz) water
950 g (33.5 oz) granulated sugar
Food colouring of your choice
Wooden skewers and glass jars

Makes: 4 sticks
Prep time: 1 hour
Cook time: none

Method

1. Take four clean, small glass jars and cut wooden skewers so they are slightly shorter than the jars. Wet the skewers with water and roll them in granulated sugar, then set them aside to dry.

2. In a medium pan, boil the water and slowly add the sugar, stirring all the time. Once all the sugar is dissolved, remove the pan from the heat.

3. Divide the sugar syrup into several bowls. Add a different food colouring to each bowl and stir well. Allow to cool slightly (10 minutes), then fill each jar with a different coloured syrup.

4. Take your prepared skewers and lower them into the jars. They musn't touch the bottom, so use a clothes-peg balanced across the top of the jar to hold them in place.

5. Transfer the jars to a cool, dark place and cover them loosely with a towel. Sugar crystals should start to grow after just a couple of hours.

6. Leave the crystals to grow as large as you'd like them – this may take a few days. Then remove from the jars, allow to dry, and enjoy.

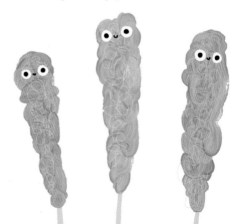